I0815383

ELECTRIC TRUCKS

Scott Wilken

Big Buddy Books
An Imprint of Abdo Publishing
abdobooks.com

abdobooks.com

Published by Abdo Publishing, a division of ABDO, PO Box 398166, Minneapolis, Minnesota 55439.

Printed in the United States of America, North Mankato, Minnesota
052023
092023

Design: Sarah DeYoung, Mighty Media, Inc.
Production: Mighty Media, Inc.
Editor: Katherine Chu
Cover Photograph: jluke/Shutterstock Images
Interior Photographs: Frank Briend/Shutterstock Images, p. 15; Jay8g/Wikimedia Commons, pp. 13, 28 (Rivian EDV); jluke/Shutterstock Images, pp. 17, 29 (Ford F-150 Lightning); Jonathan Weiss/Shutterstock Images, pp. 7, 18–19; Korbitr/Wikimedia Commons, p. 23; Kruzat/Wikimedia Commons, p. 27; Margitta Hamel/Shutterstock Images, p. 9; Michael Barera/Wikimedia Commons, pp. 5, 28 (Wood Electric Truck); Steve Jurvetson/Flickr, pp. 25, 29 (Tesla Semitruck); Victor Maschek/Shutterstock Images, p. 11; Walmart/Flickr, p. 21
Design Elements: octopusaga/Shutterstock Images (hexagon pattern); Vlad Malinovskij/Shutterstock Images (lightning bolt icon); Zoa.Arts/Shutterstock Images (lightning)

Library of Congress Control Number: 2022948823

Publisher's Cataloging-in-Publication Data
Names: Wilken, Scott, author.
Title: Electric trucks / by Scott Wilken
Description: Minneapolis, Minnesota : Abdo Publishing, 2024 | Series: It's electric! | Includes online resources and index.
Identifiers: ISBN 9781098291563 (lib. bdg.) | ISBN 9781098278021 (ebook)
Subjects: LCSH: Electric trucks--Juvenile literature. | Eco trucks--Juvenile literature. | Electric vehicles--Juvenile literature. | Transportation--Juvenile literature.
Classification: DDC 388--dc23

CONTENTS

CHAPTER 1

CLEAN & POWERFUL

Workers finish loading a truck's **trailer**. The truck driver starts the engine and drives away, easily towing several tons. The workers are amazed at how quiet it is. There are also no clouds of smoke. That's because it's an electric **vehicle** (EV)!

FAST FACT

Some electric trucks were made in the early 1900s. But gas-powered trucks cost less. So, most truck companies stopped making electric trucks.

The Wood Electric Truck was an early electric truck made in 1900 by automobile company F.R. Wood & Son.

CHAPTER 2

WHY ELECTRIC?

An EV's **motor** is powered by electricity that is stored in **batteries**. EVs are becoming popular for many reasons. Gas **vehicles release** gases that harm Earth. EVs do not. Charging an EV also costs less than buying gas.

In the 2000s, improved batteries made electric trucks fast and powerful. So, more companies are making electric trucks.

An electric truck's batteries can be charged by plugging the vehicle into an outlet or special charger.

CHAPTER 3

DELIVERY VANS

One of the fastest-growing types of electric trucks is the electric **delivery** van. In 2020, the **COVID-19 pandemic** forced people to stay at home. So, more people had **packages** delivered than ever before. This meant more delivery vans were needed!

FAST FACT

Most modern electric trucks use lithium-ion batteries.

In 2022, about one-fifth of delivery company DHL's vehicles were fully electric. DHL plans to have over 80,000 electric vehicles by 2030.

Using electric vans is one way **delivery companies** can help the **environment**. Most delivery vans stay in one city or area. This means they don't have to travel far. Most electric delivery vans can be driven for a full day on one charge. Then the **batteries** are **recharged** overnight.

FAST FACT

In 2020, gas-powered delivery **vehicles released** nearly the same amount of carbon dioxide as powering 800,000 homes for a year.

In 2021, delivery company FedEx made a promise that all of its vehicles will be electric by 2040.

Rivian is a California EV manufacturer. It is one of the leaders in making electric trucks. In 2019, American company Amazon started working with Rivian to create electric **delivery** vans. In December 2021, Rivian **released** the Rivian EDV. Amazon expects to have 100,000 Rivian EDVs on the road by 2030.

FAST FACT

A Rivian EDV has a range of 120 to 150 miles (193 to 241 km) on one charge.

Amazon has more than 1,000 Rivian EDVs in more than 100 US cities.

CHAPTER 4

PICKUP TRUCKS

Pickup trucks are another fast-growing type of electric truck. Pickups are used for **transportation**. They can **haul** boats, **trailers**, and more. Many pickup drivers want a powerful truck that doesn't **release** harmful gas.

FAST FACT

In the US, about 17 percent of all vehicles on the road are pickup trucks.

The first electric pickup to be produced was the Rivian R1T in September 2021.

Ford **Motor** Company is an **automotive** manufacturer that also makes pickup trucks. In May 2021, Ford shared details about the F-150 Lightning. It was an electric model of Ford's popular F-series of pickup trucks. The Lightning wasn't **released** until April 2022. But by the end of 2021, almost 200,000 had been reserved!

FAST FACT

The Ford F-150 Lightning was named 2023 Truck of the Year by *MotorTrend* magazine.

The Ford F-150 Lightning can be used as a backup power source. It can power a house for at least three days.

FORD F-150 LIGHTNING

Starting price: $55,974

Range: 240 miles (386 km) on one charge

Acceleration: 0 to 60 miles per hour (97 kmh) in 4.1 seconds

Towing up to: 7,700 pounds (3,493 kg)

Charging time: From 15% to 80% in 36 to 41 minutes

Statistics from 2023 PRO model

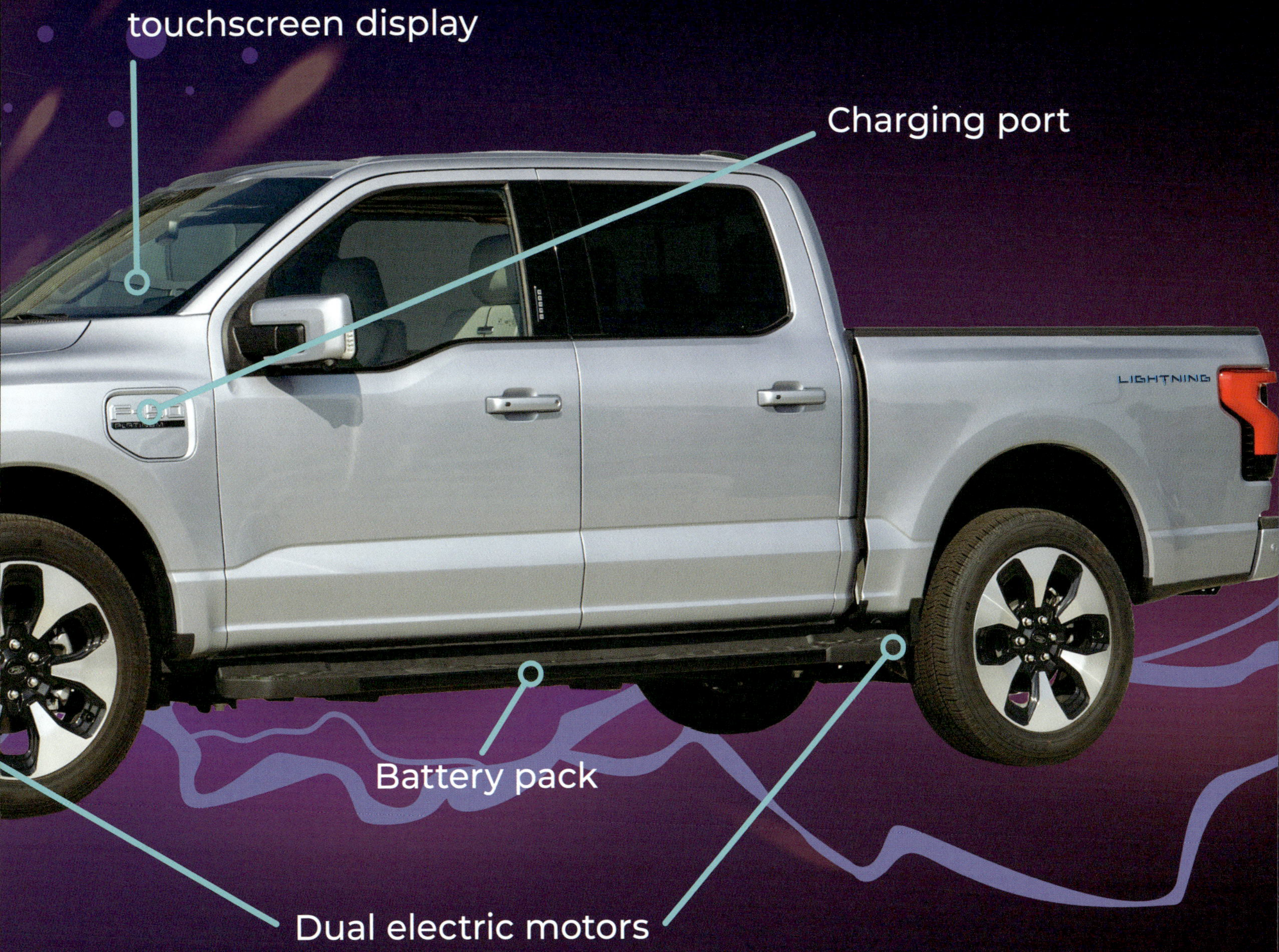
touchscreen display
Charging port
LIGHTNING
Battery pack
Dual electric motors

CHAPTER 5

SEMITRUCKS

Semitrucks are trucks that can pull large **trailers** for long distances. They **haul** food, gear, and more. Many have **diesel** engines and can travel up to 2,000 miles (3,219 km) before stopping for gas.

Until recently, EV **batteries** didn't last long enough to power semitrucks. So, diesel-powered and diesel-electric semitrucks were popular choices.

In 2010, American company Walmart used diesel-electric trucks. These created less air pollution than diesel trucks.

Several **automotive** manufacturers created electric semitrucks in 2022. But most could only drive 150 to 275 miles (241 to 443 km) between charges. So, they were used for shorter, local **deliveries**.

FAST FACT

More than 70 percent of products in the US are hauled by semitrucks.

Tesla revealed its first electric semitruck model in 2017. It began manufacturing the Tesla Semi in 2022.

The electric semitruck with the longest range is the Tesla Semi. It has three electric **motors**. This helps make the Tesla Semi powerful, fast, and able to go farther. It can drive up to 500 miles (805 km) on one charge.

American company PepsiCo ordered 36 Tesla Semis in 2017. And they have plans to buy more in 2023!

Tesla claims the Tesla Semi can save companies up to $200,000 in fuel costs over three years.

CHAPTER 6

THE FUTURE'S ELECTRIC

Many US companies are **releasing** new electric trucks. And many people believe they are useful and safe for the **environment**.

Automotive manufacturers are also continuing to improve their electric trucks. They will soon be more powerful and able to go farther. In the **future**, electric trucks may be the only kind of truck on the road!

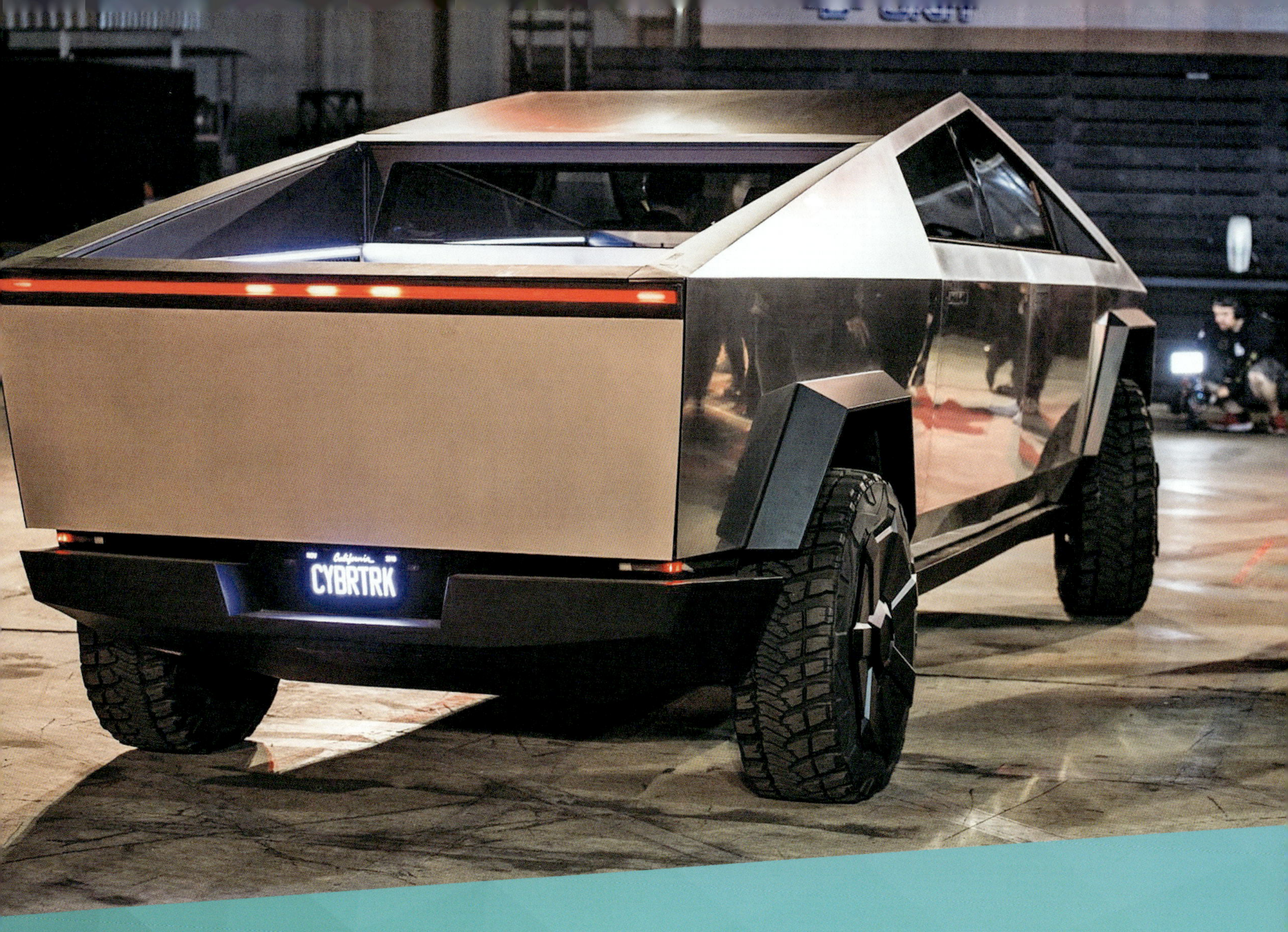

Tesla revealed its Cybertruck in 2019. It can tow up to 14,000 pounds (6,350 kg) and drive up to 500 miles (805 km) on one charge.

TIMELINE

2000s

Improved **batteries** make electric trucks fast and powerful.

2019

Amazon starts working with EV manufacturer Rivian to create the Rivian EDV.

EARLY 1900s

Some electric trucks are made, but they cost more than gas-powered trucks.

2020

The **COVID-19 pandemic** leads to increased home **deliveries**.

2021

Ford **Motor** Company reveals the F-150 Lightning pickup truck. Almost 200,000 of them are reserved by the end of the year.

2022

Ford **releases** the F-150 Lightning. Tesla starts manufacturing the Tesla Semi.

GLOSSARY

acceleration (ihk-seh-luh-RAY-shuhn)—the act of increasing in speed.

automotive—relating to or concerned with motor vehicles.

battery—a small container filled with chemicals that makes electrical power.

COVID-19 pandemic—the outbreak of an infectious disease caused by the SARS-CoV-2 virus that spread quickly over a large area.

deliver—to take something somewhere or to someone. Delivery is the process of taking something somewhere or to someone.

diesel—a fuel designed for use in diesel engines.

environment—the natural world, including air, water, land, and animals.

future (FYOO-chuhr)—a time that has not yet occurred.

haul—to transport in a vehicle.

lithium-ion battery—a rechargeable battery that uses lithium ions as the primary component.

motor—a machine that produces motion or power for doing work.

package—an item that has been wrapped or placed in a box.

recharge—to become charged again.

release—to let go or make available to the public.

trailer—an unpowered vehicle towed by another.

transportation—the act of moving people or things from one place to another.

vehicle—something used for carrying persons or large objects. Some examples of vehicles are cars, trucks, boats, and airplanes.

ONLINE RESOURCES

To learn more about electric trucks, visit abdobooklinks.com. These links are routinely monitored and updated to provide the most current information available.

INDEX